JOY
BEYOND
THE PAGE

a scripture study for
DISCOVERING JOY
EVERY DAY

CHANTAL JOHNSON

LUCIDBOOKS

Joy Beyond the Page
A Scripture Study for Discovering Joy Every Day
Copyright © 2025 by Chantal Johnson

Published by Lucid Books in Houston, TX
www.LucidBooks.com

Unless otherwise indicated, scripture quotations are taken from the NIV (the Holy Bible, New International Version®.) Copyright ©1973, 1978, 1983, 1984, 2011 by Biblica, Inc.™ Used by permission of Zondervan. All rights reserved worldwide. www.zondervan.com The "NIV" and "New International Version" are trademarks registered in the United States Patent and Trademark Office by Biblica, Inc.™

Scripture quotations marked (CEB) are from the Common English Bible®, CEB® Copyright © 2010, 2011 by Common English Bible.™ Used by permission. All rights reserved worldwide.

Scripture quotations marked (CEV) are from the Contemporary English Version Copyright © 1991, 1992, 1995 by American Bible Society, Used by Permission.

Scripture quotations marked (ERV) are taken from the HOLY BIBLE: EASY-TO-READ VERSION © 2001 by World Bible Translation Center, Inc. and used by permission. All rights reserved.

Scripture quotations marked (ESV) are taken from the ESV® Bible (The Holy Bible, English Standard Version®), copyright © 2001 by Crossway, a publishing ministry of Good News Publishers. Used by permission. All rights reserved.

Scripture quotations marked (GNT) are from the Good News Translation in Today's English Version- Second Edition Copyright © 1992 by American Bible Society. Used by Permission.

Scripture quotations marked (HCSB) are taken from the Holman Christian Standard Bible®, Copyright © 1999, 2000, 2002, 2003, 2009 by Holman Bible Publishers. Used by permission. Holman Christian Standard Bible®, Holman CSB®, and HCSB® are federally registered trademarks of Holman Bible Publishers.

Scripture quotations marked (KJV) are taken from the King James Version (KJV): King James Version, public domain.
Scripture quotations marked (NKJV) are taken from the New King James Version®. Copyright © 1982 by Thomas Nelson. Used by permission. All rights reserved.

Scripture quotations marked (NLT) are taken from the Holy Bible, New Living Translation, copyright ©1996, 2004, 2015 by Tyndale House Foundation. Used by permission of Tyndale House Publishers, Carol Stream, Illinois 60188. All rights reserved.

Scripture quotations marked (TPT) are from The Passion Translation®. Copyright © 2017, 2018, 2020 by Passion & Fire Ministries, Inc. Used by permission. All rights reserved. ThePassionTranslation.com.

ISBN: 978-1-63296-844-9
eISBN: 978-1-63296-845-6

Special Sales: Most Lucid Books titles are available in special quantity discounts. Custom imprinting or excerpting can also be done to fit special needs. Contact Lucid Books at Info@LucidBooks.com

To my husband, Scott: Thank you for the joy you have brought to my life. Your love is constant and unwavering. Your generosity knows no limit, and your laughter is contagious. You have given me courage to follow what God has placed on my heart and grace as I make a few more trips to Hobby Lobby, the store filled with joy.

Who knew what joy would come from a simple question: "Is your name Devon?" Thank you for finding out my name, so I could one day take yours.
With joy, I thank the Lord for you!

"Chantal's gift is language. All words. She can interpret a meaning in a single word that teaches our weekly Bible study to understand scripture in a new hue. She enthusiastically encourages us to read a variety of the dozens of published Bible translations in our app so that each of us can find one specific translation whose words sing to our own unique hearts. I'm blessed to spend time with her each week."

—Maire Anders,
Homemaker, Rowlett, Texas

"Chantal has an amazing gift of hospitality and a love for sharing God's word. I have been blessed to attend her Bible studies and always look forward to studying with such a sweet soul."

—Desirée Terrell,
Wife and Mother, Rockwall, Texas

"I have had the privilege of being a member of Chantal Johnson's studies for the last several years. Chantal has a gift of engaging the reader well beyond completing the Bible study; her heart is evident to the participant. The love and prayers that are poured into every page will captivate you. Chantal carefully researches, plans, and produces her studies to engage you at multiple levels. And I am looking forward to *Joy Beyond the Page* and the opportunity to discover His joy in our everyday."

—Donna Duren,
Certified Professional Life Coach , Rowlett, Texas

"Chantal is an excellent teacher. She knows her scriptures and offers different translations to help us have more insight into what God wants us to learn. She has the gift of hospitality and graciously makes everyone feel welcome and accepted."

—Paula Cannon,
Teacher and Friend, Rowlett, Texas

"Chantal Johnson radiates joy and—in this study—you get to see where her joy comes from: her relationship with our Savior."

—Patti Tamez,
Rowlett, Texas

TABLE OF CONTENTS

DISCOVERING JOY EVERY DAY

May the God of hope fill you with all joy and peace as you trust in him, so that you may overflow with the hope by the power of the Holy Spirit.

—Romans 15:13

A s I write this Bible study, I am sitting in a sweet café in West Branch, Iowa, where the town's motto is "Where Friends Meet." This is where I find myself in the pages of Scripture—where friends meet, where we together uncover the ingredients of a life made lovely by Jesus, who is not only our Savior (though that is more than enough), but He is also our friend who is closer than a brother. He invites us to meet Him in the pages of Scripture where we also meet friends from ages past. Like us, they longed for joy to be served and savored and then shared with others who may not know that true, deep joy can be found in Him. And when we read the timeless words, we experience joy, immeasurable and unending. We find joy in the messes and in the mornings, in the daily and yes, even in the disappointments. This is the joy that transcends circumstance, chaos, and culture. This is the joy promised and present in our faith.

In this study, we will find that joy is expressed and audible; it is movable and discoverable—a joy that is served in every season and in every situation. This is not the world's joy; rather, it is the heavenly joy that comes to dwell in our hearts and is seen in our lives through the holy living Spirit of God Himself. It is the fruit that is produced in our lives because we are planted in the soil of the Spirit.

Back to the café: The owners' motto is "Living on Grace and Coffee." Oh, and the name of the cafe is The Serving Café. So, sweet friend, with joy on our minds, let's pour a cup of coffee, sit together, and open our hearts and the pages of Scripture to discover the joy that is best served with Jesus.

INTRODUCTION

There is joy to be found in our gatherings.

CREATIVE GATHERINGS, PLANS, AND PROJECTS

Join me for a study and gathering where the love of God, His word, and the love of all things creative combine for an evening of Bible study, inspiration, and fun while we share and create beautiful reminders of His love for us.

This is how I start every invitation for family, friends, and those who will become friends. As one who loves studying and sharing God's word, I love to open the doors of my home and my heart to those who love the Lord, love art, love food, and need a place to belong. All are welcome in my home. And to you, my dear reader, welcome to this study, *Joy Beyond the Page*.

Come join me for a journey through Scripture as we discover the true abiding joy that is found in following Jesus and in the faithful promises of God. We will open the pages of Scripture to find timeless truths and confident hope when we grab hold of the good news of the gospel and the goodness of our God. This joy will infuse our lives with praise and purpose. And as we see that this joy is protected, we will have no fear of someone or something robbing us of our joy. This is a six-week Scripture study that will take us from Old Testament writers to the writers of the early church, from Solomon's wise words to the words of Jesus. And our greatest discovery will be that the joy we seek is Jesus who is the "Joy Beyond the Page."

CREATIVE STUDY FOR INDIVIDUALS

- Gather all your materials such as your Bible, *Joy Beyond the Page*, highlighter, pen, commentary (if desired, but not needed). Place them all in a basket or a bag, so that all your materials are ready when you are.
- Find a place in your home or wherever you choose to study that is beautiful to you. Pleasant surroundings can be a catalyst to help you stay focused and linger over His word.
- Read Scripture verses in more than one translation; different Bible versions can prompt new thoughts— especially with familiar Scripture passages. A different version can spark an image or a nuance for a verse that you may have read over and over again.
- Find a daily rhythm and establish a time that works in your everyday routine.
- Each day's study begins with "Daily Joy in His Word," which gives the verse for the day. Write the verse and then follow the other prompts and write as much as you can about the specific focus area for that day and record your observations. (See "The Daily Ingredients to Study

His Word" below.) When we read and write the words of Scripture, our minds grab hold of them and bring them into our thoughts and speech throughout the day, which then creates greater impact in our lives. If you only have a short amount of time, I encourage you to write the verse because His word is the most important part of this study.

CREATIVE STUDY WITH GROUPS

If you are leading or facilitating a small group or gathering, consider using a few of these ideas to create an atmosphere that is welcoming to all and that serves as a reminder of His love and His word.

- Pray first! Pray for God to be ever present in you and in your group. Pray that His word will be received and loved more every day. Pray for each person in your group by name and pray that all come to know Jesus. Ask for His love to be evident to all. Pray for a fresh word from the timeless word of God.
- Name tags! Print, make, or write name tags every week; this is an easy way to ensure that each member of the group is known. Having names tags means that newcomers won't feel pressure to memorize everyone's name.
- If you are leading a gathering in a home, serve refreshments or invite others to participate in bringing refreshments. Be sure to allow time for people to get to know one another. This can be a shared responsibility, but never underestimate the importance of hospitality—it creates an inviting atmosphere for everyone.
- Create a bookmark for each member or have each member create their own, to be used throughout the study. The

bookmark can be as simple as cardstock with a printed verse—whatever your creativity, time, and resources permit. I have used a variety of bookmarks from beaded bookmarks to laminated notepaper to large paperclips with tassels. Choose symbols such as hearts to carry out the theme of the study.

- Print verse card downloads to be given to each small group member each week. When I prepare for the studies that I teach, I prepare a Scripture bag that includes the study guide, a highlighter, a pen, Week 1 verse cards, and a bookmark for each member of the group. (Verse cards for this study are available at chantaljohnsonauthor.com.)

For each following week, I prepare the verse cards for that week and add a small item, which serves as a reminder of one of the verses. For example, I might include pineapple candy (i.e., hospitality), a small vial of bubbles (i.e., His word bubbles over), a flower seed packet (i.e., the word of God is planted), or a spur charm (i.e., let us spur one another on to good works), and so on. This is a way to add reminders of God in our daily lives. Keep tokens simple and only do what you can do; remember that the intention of your heart is to help share the goodness of God's word in tangible ways.

- Feel free to lead the group in doing art projects that come from the verses themselves—whatever will help participants grasp what is spoken of or taught in the verses. For example, when I taught on the armor of God, we made belt bracelet cuffs from vintage belts and snaps using a snap setter.

SUGGESTED TIMELINE FOR GROUP STUDY

The facilitator or group leader has the following responsibilities.

Week 1 – Introduction
- Distribute *Joy Beyond the Page* (include a Scripture bag, if possible).
- Share refreshments or a meal and allow time for the group to get to know one another.
- Give an overview of the study and review the format for each day along with the overall schedule for your study.
- Remind everyone that what is shared in the group stays in the group; remind them to only share what they are comfortable sharing.
- Encourage participation.
- If you choose to use creative reminders, create a bookmark or verse holder.

Weeks 2–7
- Distribute verse cards (and reminders, if possible).
- Share and review the previous week's study activities.
- Share refreshments or a meal and allow time for group discussion.

THE DAILY INGREDIENTS TO STUDY HIS WORD

Each day's study includes time for the following focus areas: Finding joy in His word, adding joy to our walk, and sharing joy in our world. Each day, the author shares insights about finding joy in daily worship and in our daily whispers to God in prayer.

Daily Joy in His Word: From the Scripture, write out the verse of the day. If needed, use different Bible translations to help you see the Scripture with fresh eyes.

Daily Joy in My Walk: Think of ways to infuse joy into your day. What is the verse teaching or revealing about the joy from His word? Record your observations.

Daily Joy in My World: Consider how you can bring His joy to others. What practical applications can you use to share this joy? Write things you can do now and perhaps some things you can grow into later.

Daily Joy in Our Worship: Read the author's reflections on what His word teaches and where His joy is leading us.

Daily Joy in My Whispers: Participate in a moment of prayer recorded each day. You may use the prayer that is provided or write a prayer of your own. The Lord longs to hear from us.

JOY JOURNAL

Each week's study ends with a space to record what has filled you with joy, what has stolen your joy, and who has received your joy. Consider these prompts:

- What has filled you with joy? This can be a fresh word from your time in God's word, a word from a friend, time with your family, and so on.
- What has stolen your joy? This may be annoyances, arguments, anxiousness, or anything that has weighed you down. Once you are aware of these joy stealers, you can fight back with praise, prayer, and people who encourage you.
- Who has received your joy? This is where you get to live out the Joy of the Lord. Who did you encourage, embrace, or encounter that received blessings from you, either in word or action?

DISCOVERING JOY IN EVERY DAY (DAYS 1–30)

WEEK 1 DAILY PLAN

Day 1 – Joy is promised.

Day 2 – Joy is proven.

Day 3 – Joy is protected.

Day 4 – Joy is present with peace.

Day 5 – Joy Journal.

Joy in Our Anxious Moments

WEEK 2 DAILY PLAN

Day 6 – Joy comes from His love.

Day 7 – Joy comes from His word.

Day 8 – Joy comes from His presence.

Day 9 – Joy comes from His purpose.

Day 10– Joy Journal.

Joy Comes in the Morning

WEEK 3 DAILY PLAN

Day 11 – Joy in walking in the word.

Day 12 – Joy in walking in today.

Day 13 – Joy in walking in the light.

Day 14 – Joy in walking in step with the Spirit.

Day 15 – Joy Journal.

Joy in Our Wardrobe

WEEK 4 DAILY PLAN

Day 16 – Joy brings hope.

Day 17 – Joy brings comfort.

Day 18 – Joy brings confidence.

Day 19 – Joy brings celebration.

Day 20 – Joy Journal.

WEEK 5 DAILY PLAN

Day 21 – Joy is found in God's good news.

Day 22 – Joy is found in God's people.

Day 23 – Joy is found in God's goodness.

Day 24 – Joy is found in God's generosity and our gratitude.

Day 25 – Joy Journal.

WEEK 6 DAILY PLAN

Day 26 – Joy knows to speak.

Day 27 – Joy knows to sing.

Day 28 – Joy knows to share.

Day 29 – Joy knows to serve.

Day 30 – Joy Journal.

Joy in Our Celebration (Psalm 100)

Joy Reminders

GETTING STARTED

Sometimes, Bible studies, like recipes, can be cumbersome. When we embark on a new recipe, we look at the ingredient list, sometimes noticing that the list seems longer than the line for entrance into Disney World. Some recipes take hours or even days to make. If our time is limited, we have to make a decision: Do we make the dish from scratch or go for the store-bought version?

Let's apply a similar approach to studying God's word. All you need are basic ingredients that you have on hand; the time and effort that you put in will be well worth it. The result of your study will be a sweet aroma to the Lord—like that of homemade cookies, fresh from the oven. Our first ingredient is a willing heart that desires to hear from God through His word. Next on the list is a warm, inviting place to sit and study—think of a place in which you draw inspiration—a place that promotes reflection. You will need a few more ingredients, such as your Bible, a pen, and this book. Finally, add to those ingredients time, prayer, and purpose—prayer to center our hearts and purpose to give us intention with direction.

Take a moment to set the direction for this study and then identify or create a set place and time that will bring joy to your heart. Take a few minutes to record your initial goals and desires for this study:

- My Goals:

- My Heart's Desires and Direction:

1.

2.

3.

WEEK 1

DAY 1

Your promises are the source of my bubbling joy; the revelations of your Word thrills me like one who has discovered hidden treasure.

—Psalm 119:162 TPT

*As the rain and the snow come down from heaven, and do not return to it without watering the earth and making it bud and flourish, so that it yields seed for the sower and bread for the eater, so is **my word** that goes out from my mouth: It will not return to me empty, but will accomplish what I desire and achieve the purpose for which I sent it. **You will go out in joy and be led forth in peace;** the mountains and hills will burst into song before you, and all the trees of the field will clap their hands.*

—Isaiah 55:10–12, emphasis added

Instead of your shame you will receive a double portion, and instead of disgrace you will rejoice in your inheritance. And so you will inherit a double portion in your land, and everlasting joy will be yours.

—Isaiah 61:7

DAY 1 – JOY IS PROMISED.

Daily Joy in His word: Isaiah 55:12

Daily Joy in my walk:

DAY 1 - JOY IS PROMISED.

Daily Joy in my world:

DAY 1 – JOY IS PROMISED.

Daily Joy in our worship:

God promises that we can have joy at the end of our captivity and that His peace will lead the way; these are promises that we can still claim today. While we may not experience physical captivity as in the time of Isaiah, we can still be held captive. Sometimes, the captivity we experience is due to our own choices or the choices of others. Sometimes, it is a consequence of our sin or of the brokenness of our world. And for others, it is the captivity of addiction or trauma. Regardless of the type of captivity, there is a greater power to rescue and redeem us: Jesus. When He frees us from the weight of sin and death and when He releases us from the hold of captivity, there is joy! Isaiah says that there will be joy after captivity. Paul writes that there can be joy during captivity. These are promises to take hold of—that in either situation, He saves and sets us free!

Daily Joy in my whispers:

Lord, Your promise of joy in the midst of captivity, gives us strength and hope in the hard moments—strength to remain steadfast and hope in the certainty that You will bring freedom and peace. May this promise of joy be a testimony of Your salvation because You always save. With Jesus, we know we are free. With joy, we pray in Jesus' name. Amen.

DAY 2

Consider it pure joy, my brothers, whenever you face [surrounded with] *trials of many kinds, because you know that the testing of your faith develops perseverance* [cheerful hope, endurance]. *Perseverance must finish its work so that you may be mature and complete* [in every part], *not lacking in anything.*

—James 1:2–4

These troubles [trials] *test your faith and prove that it is pure. And such faith is worth more than gold. Gold can be proved to be pure by fire* **but** *gold will ruin. When your faith is proven to be pure, the result will be praise and glory and honor when Jesus Christ comes. You have not seen Christ* **but** *still love him. You can't see him now,* **but** *you believe in him. You are filled with a* **wonderful and heavenly joy that can't be explained**. *Your faith* [fidelity, assurance] *has a goal and you are reaching that goal—your salvation.*

—1 Peter 1:7–9 ERV, emphasis added

DAY 2 – JOY IS PROVEN.

Daily Joy in His word: 1 Peter 1:8–9

Daily Joy in my walk:

DAY 2 – JOY IS PROVEN.

Daily Joy in my world:

DAY 2 – JOY IS PROVEN.

Daily Joy in our worship:

The joy expressed in 1 Peter 1:8–9 comes from a proven faith that chooses to believe and follow Jesus, no matter the heat or the size of the fire. Gold can ruin even after it has been refined, but with Jesus, our refining joy remains. James teaches us to set our minds and our hearts on joy when we encounter all kinds of trials and troubles. Trials may seem long, and they may try our resolve. Sometimes, troubles are the sudden storms that shake us and cause us to shift our foundation. We need wisdom to get through those times. We need to know that depending on the depth of our faith, we will develop either a cheerful hope with perseverance or bitterness and doubt. When you go through trials, ask the Lord, "What am I learning?" Where can I find joy? Who and where can I serve?" When I have asked these questions, He has been faithful to answer. He will do the same for you.

My faith, tested and genuine, will deepen and bring praise, glory, and honor to God. My faith, tested and genuine, develops perseverance and endurance in me to continue to do the next right thing. The heavenly joy we receive in these hard times and heavy places is a joy that is not understood by an earthly mind. With Jesus, there is joy because we know without a doubt that all things work for our good and His glory (recognition of who He is and His worth), because we know that He will never leave us, nor forsake us; He remains close to the brokenhearted, and He loves us perfectly. Joy comes from knowing that He is with us always and that nothing can separate us from His love. With Jesus, as our wisdom, we set our minds and hearts on Him who set the joys of home and Heaven before Him and endured the cross, so that we could live a heavenly joy-filled life.

Daily Joy in my whispers:

Lord,

In the hard times and heavy places, may we reach for Your word, which proclaims that there is joy in enduring. You have given us heavenly joy that transcends where we are and what is happening to us. With Your word in our hearts, we can say that You are with us, You are for us, and You are near to us. This is all that we need to see that Your joy is proven over and over in our lives. May we set the joys of home and Heaven in our hearts and live a life of joy in You. With joy, we pray in Jesus' name. Amen

DAY 3

But all who find safety in you will rejoice; they can always sing for joy. Protect those who love you; because of you, they are truly happy.

—Psalm 5:11 GNT

"A woman giving birth to a child has pain because her time has come; but when her baby is born she forgets the anguish because of her joy that a child is born into the world. So with you: Now is your time of grief, but I will see you again and you will rejoice, and no one will take away your joy."

—John 16:21–22

And at times you were publicly and shamefully mistreated, being persecuted for your faith; then at other times you stood side by side with those who preach the message of hope. You sympathized with those in prison and when all your belongings were confiscated you accepted this violation with joy; convinced that you possess a treasure growing in heaven that could never be taken from you. *So don't lose your bold, courageous faith, for you are destined for a great reward!*

—Hebrews 10:33–35 TPT, emphasis added

DAY 3 – JOY IS PROTECTED.

Daily Joy in His word: Psalm 5:11

Daily Joy in my walk:

DAY 3 – JOY IS PROTECTED.

Daily Joy in my world:

DAY 3 - JOY IS PROTECTED.

Daily Joy in our worship:

Under the Lord's protection, I can have joy in all situations. No one or nothing can steal my joy without my permission. Knowing that I am safe from the world's chaos; from condemnation; and from being left alone, forsaken, or forgotten, I am able to receive the security of a sure word, a sure foundation and a sure heavenly Father who protects and provides joy. Learning from Jesus (Hebrews 12:2), I can say for the joy of Heaven set before me:

> I can endure insults and persecution.
> I can endure ridicule and hardship.
> I can even endure loss.

Sharing His safety with words of certainty, compassion, and care, I create a melody that sings a song of joy. By living a faith-forward life that is secure, joyful, loving, kind, happy, and content, I am able share His love as the reason for my happiness. Eternal joy, protected by the Father and given through Jesus who is my greater reward, is kept safely in Heaven while He keeps me safe here.

Daily Joy in my whispers:

> Lord,
>
> In moments of instability and uncertainty, may we seek and find safety in You as it is promised in Your word. Give us joyful words that come from a joyful heart, knowing that our greater joy is kept safe in Your home. We know that You give joy to all who love You; Lord, we rejoice and are happy because of Your great love for us. With joy, we pray, in Jesus' name. Amen.

DAY 4

Deceit fills hearts that are plotting evil; joy fills hearts that are planting peace!

—Proverbs 12:20 NLT

"I have told you these things, so that in me you may have peace. In this world you will have trouble. But take heart, I have overcome the world."

—John 16:33

DAY 4 – JOY IS PRESENT WITH PEACE.

Daily Joy in His word: Proverbs 12:20

Daily Joy in my walk:

DAY 4 – JOY IS PRESENT WITH PEACE.

Daily Joy in my world:

DAY 4 - JOY IS PRESENT WITH PEACE.

Daily Joy in our worship:

Plotting or planting? The first thing that came to my mind when reading this verse was the continual conniving of the Pharisees recorded in Mark 3. After Jesus healed a man with a shriveled hand, the Pharisees were silent, and their hearts were stubborn. They could find no joy, no peace, no gratitude for this man's complete restoration. Then they left, and they plotted.

Although people may not connive murderous plots, there are those who spend their time plotting on how to get ahead, how to get away with something, or how to get out of something. Deceit is filling up their stubborn hearts and spilling out into their lives; they are calculating each transaction, each encounter, and looking for the easy way out. When evil is the plot, deceit is the product. The result is a hurried, weary, chaotic, and in-it-for-me, ever-changing life. Proverbs 12:20 also highlights the beautiful opportunity we have for planting. When we plant our hearts in the rich soil of God's word, we find that the Living Water is flowing with everything we need to flourish with joy and peace. Jesus gives us His shalom, which is every kind of blessing that brings peace, prosperity, wholeness, and rest—ultimately, the peace that brings a reconciled right relationship with God and sets us at one with Him. Our joy is complete when we remain in Him. Our hearts and our minds will find joy when peace is our aim—not just the absence of conflict—but the presence of the One who is the answer to our struggle. The Lord knows that joy grows best in hearts where the seeds of peace and the good news of the gospel are sown. What are you planting? No matter the season, peace is always available.

Daily Joy in my whispers:

Lord,

May our plans always point to Jesus who is our peace. May we plant a deep garden of peace in our lives, and may we give from the bounty we receive to those who are in need of Your peace, Your joy, and Your salvation. May we be ever joyful that we are Your friends and that Your peace comforts and Your joy completes us. With joy, we pray in Jesus' name. Amen.

DAY 5

JOY JOURNAL

Use the space below to record your insights about joy this week:

- What has filled you with joy? This can be a fresh word from your time in God's word, a word from a friend, time with your family, and so on.
- What has stolen your joy? This can be annoyances, arguments, anxiety, or anything that has weighed you down. Once you are aware of these joy stealers, you can fight back with praise, prayer, and people who encourage you.
- Who has received your joy? This is where you get to live out the Joy of the Lord. Who did you encourage, embrace, or encounter that received blessings from you, either in word or action?

Joy fillers:

Joy stealers:

Joy receivers:

JOY IN OUR ANXIOUS MOMENTS

When I said, "My foot is slipping," your unfailing love,
LORD, supported me. When anxiety was great within
me, your consolation brought me joy.

—Psalm 94:18–19

What do we do when anxious thoughts come into our mind and anxious moments come into our life? The psalmist said that these thoughts were multiplying at a rapid pace. Have you ever been there—when one anxious thought leads to another anxious thought and another and another and what was once only one thought has multiplied beyond what you can bear? We may feel that we are slipping down a slippery slope of what-ifs. And while we know that not one of the things we fear has come to pass, we need something to hold onto and to hope for, something to bring us joy.

The psalmist gives us the remedy for those anxious moments when we find ourselves in those not so steady places. The answer lies in the Lord's unfailing love and His consolation, His comfort, His solace, and His compassion. He strengthens, establishes, and refreshes us. What does His compassion look like? How does He establish us? I believe the best place to find the answer to these questions is in His word, which shows us the way to move from anxiousness to assurance, from jostling about to abundant joy. Psalm 119 tells us that our delight is found in the Lord's decrees and commands—His holy word. When we hide His word in our hearts, we can speak life and hope, faith and vitality into our conversations and circumstances. He establishes our hearts, centering them on Jesus, guiding us by the Holy Spirit, to learn and to love His word. His compassion comes through new mornings, new mercies, new perspectives, and new purposes as well as through trusted friends and wise counselors.

While He does this, what do we do? We begin to replace those anxious thoughts with comforts and promises from His word. Here is an "assurance list" to get you started. As you ponder these assurances, watch how the what-ifs disappear and the "what is" begins to appear in your thoughts and in your moments.

- He is the God of all comfort.
- His love is everlasting.
- He is my Shepherd; I lack nothing.
- Nothing can separate me from His love.
- He surrounds me with His favor.
- He sings over me with joy.
- He protects me, provides for me.
- He works everything out for my good and His glory.
- His mercies are new every morning.
- I have Jesus—my savior, redeemer, and friend.
- He has given me grace upon grace.
- He equips me for every good work that He has prepared for me, gives good gifts, and fills my life with good things.
- His goodness and love will follow me all the days of my life.
- I have the indwelling of the Holy Spirit.
- I have a Spirit of power, love, and self-control.
- I can take hold of my thoughts and infuse them with the love and power of Jesus.
- I am to think on what is lovely, pure, true, excellent, admirable, right, and praiseworthy.
- I walk in faith, not fear. I walk in the present, not in the future.
- No matter where I walk, I stand in His grace.

Keep adding to this list and watch joy grow in your heart as anxiousness is replaced with assurance.

WEEK 2

DAY 6

If you keep my commands, you will remain in my love, just as I have kept my Father's command and remain in his love. I have told you this so that my joy may be in you and that your joy may be complete. My command is this: Love each other as I have loved you."

—John 15:10–12

Love the LORD your God, with all your heart and with all your soul and with all your strength. These commandments that I give you today are to be on your hearts.

—Deuteronomy 6:5

DAY 6 – JOY COMES FROM HIS LOVE.

Daily Joy in His word: John 15:11

Daily Joy in my walk:

DAY 6 – JOY COMES FROM HIS LOVE.

Daily Joy in my world:

DAY 6 – JOY COMES FROM HIS LOVE.

Daily Joy in our worship:

God teaches us wisdom in the secret places (Psalm 139). Jesus shares the secret to having joy, complete joy. In his letter to the Philippians, Paul shares the secret to having contentment (Philippians 4:13). Some secrets are worth sharing. Jesus whispers to us that the secret to joy is found in Him. His love was perfectly demonstrated on the cross; therefore, we are to remain in Him and keep His commands, which are not burdensome but are for our benefit. He is gracious to give us the commands; they are not mysterious, nor are they hidden. We do not have to guess what to do. His words are the truth and are trustworthy. His love brings complete joy when I keep His commands. The secret is out: Love God and love people the way that Jesus did. If we love as He commanded, we will have joy. As we remain in His love, our obedience brings joy. We will love better, trust more, and obey more; our hearts will be filled with deep, abiding joy. And that is a secret worth sharing!

Daily Joy in my whispers:

Lord,

May we seek contentment through Your word and not through the ways of the world. May we know that with You we have everything we need, contrary to what the world would have us believe. We have been equipped to do the very things You have done; we have enough, more than enough, when we follow Your way and Your word. May we, like Paul, share the joy and contentment we find in Jesus and His love. With joy, we pray in Jesus' name. Amen.

DAY 7

Nehemiah said, "Go and enjoy choice food and sweet drinks, and send some to those who have nothing prepared. This day is holy to our Lord. Do not grieve, for the joy of the Lord is your strength."

—Nehemiah 8:10

When I discovered your words I devoured them. They are my joy and my heart's delight, for I bear your name, O Lord God of Heaven's Armies.

—Jeremiah 15:16 NLT

I consider your Word to be my greatest treasure, and I treasure it in my heart to keep me from committing sin's treason against you.

—Psalm 119:11 TPT

DAY 7 – JOY COMES FROM HIS WORD.

Daily Joy in His word: Jeremiah 15:16

Daily Joy in my walk:

DAY 7 - JOY COMES FROM HIS WORD.

Daily Joy in my world:

DAY 7 - JOY COMES FROM HIS WORD.

Daily Joy in our worship:

As I sit and think on these passages from Nehemiah and Jeremiah, before me is a beignet aux bluet from Tim Horton's in Canada. Translated, it's a blueberry fritter, or another translation [mine] might read, "full of joy and, of course, sugar." My choice morsel, if you will. What could be better?

In our Scriptures for today, both Nehemiah and Jeremiah give us another recipe for joy. Nehemiah records that after the reading of God's word, the people wept with godly sorrow, but it was time to worship and celebrate with rich drinks, sweet food (no mention of broccoli, kale, or peas—praise the Lord!). It was time to share with those who had nothing. He tells the people to stop the grieving; it's time for joy, contagious joy! There is joy to be received when we read and understand His word. We celebrate with great joy, great food, and great company as we learn His word, together. This is perhaps the first recording of what we might call a fellowship dinner, dinner on the grounds, or a church potluck.

We experience generosity when we read and celebrate His word. His word causes our hearts and our hands to be open and ready. We cannot hold onto guilt as we pass the plate of forgiveness, nor can we continue to drink bitterness when He has given us living water. Jeremiah says that God's words are so good that he ate them, not with reservation but with joy, and they became his heart's delight. He knew that having God's word in his heart and in his life would bring him into the family of God. When we savor every word on the pages of Scripture, when we drink deeply of the words from Jesus, we gain security, rest, freedom, salvation, life principles, peace, grace, mercy, provision, certainty, the pathway, restoration, and the hope of Heaven. And that's just the beginning.

What I fill my physical body with will either fuel my energy or drain my vitality. This blueberry fritter will not sustain me, but God's word will. Being in His word fills my heart with joy, happiness, energy, and vitality. And when I fill my heart with His word, I will speak with joy, delight, blessings, and wisdom. How do we fill our hearts? By meditating, reflecting, writing, and reading His word. Let us begin a healthy habit of feasting on His word daily—perhaps with a blueberry fritter and a cup of coffee in hand.

Daily Joy in my whispers:

Lord,

May we hunger and thirst for righteousness, for the fruit of the Spirit, for the Bread of Life and the Living water. May we desire Your every word so that we are filled to overflowing and satisfied, not with delectables that are of this world but with the delicacies of Your grace, mercy, and loving-kindness. May our daily joy intake be full of the richness of Your word and perhaps an occasional blueberry fritter. With joy, we pray in Jesus' name. Amen.

DAY 8

*We wait in hope for the Lord; he is our help and shield.
In him our hearts rejoice, for we trust in his holy name.
May your unfailing love be with us, Lord, even as we put
our hope in you.*

—Psalm 33:20–22

*But may all who see you rejoice and be glad in you; may
those who long for your saving help always say, "The
Lord is great!"*

—Psalm 70:4

*To this John replied, "A person can receive only what is
given from heaven. You yourselves can testify that I said,
'I am not the Messiah but am sent ahead of him.' The
bride belongs to the bridegroom. The friend who attends
the bridegroom waits and listens for him, and is full of
joy when he hears the bridegroom's voice. That joy is
mine, and it is now complete.*

—John 3:28–30

*"Very truly I tell you, you will weep and mourn while the
world rejoices. You will grieve, but your grief will turn to joy."*

—John 16:20

DAY 8 – J OY COMES FROM HIS PRESENCE.

Daily Joy in His word: Psalm 33:20–22, John 16:20

Daily Joy in my walk:

DAY 8 – J OY COMES FROM HIS PRESENCE.

Daily Joy in my world:

DAY 8 – JOY COMES FROM HIS PRESENCE.

Daily Joy in our worship:

Are you all in? In hope? In Him? In His holy name? Are you ready to experience grief that seems like there is no joy to be found? Are you ready to wait a little while for the Lord to turn your grief into joy? Are you trusting in His word and in His ways? The disciples were all in—sort of. They were all in when it was easy, when it was going according to their plans, when hope was right there in their midst. All in when the name of Jesus was mentioned with praise for their rabbi, their teacher, their Lord. Were they ready for grief, the kind of overwhelming grief that literally turned their day to night? The answer quite simply is no, and neither are we.

The disciples didn't have the rest of the story; they didn't know about Resurrection Sunday. But we do. They waited and waited after His death . . . three long dark days; they were isolated, perhaps wondering why, how, and what was next. They experienced the predicted grief, but they forgot His promise of their joy returning—a joy that would not—could not be taken away. In the depth of their grief, the possibility of joy was unimaginable and incomprehensible for the eleven and those with them. Then He came to them in their grief, in their loneliness, and in their disbelief. Christ came. Joy came. Courage came. And perhaps, they gained a deeper understanding of His words spoken to them before the cross.

When we sit in grief and sorrow, it can seem unimaginable and incomprehensible that our joy will return. When I am in the dark, feeling isolated, full of questions, and wondering what is next, Jesus comes. Joy comes. Courage comes. He sees me, considers me, and delivers me. At times, He comes in the whispers the Holy Spirit places in our minds. Or He comes when we hear the very words we need from a godly influence in our lives. And for me always, He leaps off the pages of Scripture. The Lord brings to you and to me the word of His unfailing love. The earth is full of His unfailing love—from the air we breathe to the sunrise and sunset of each day to the ground we walk upon and to those who walk with us. In His presence we have fullness of joy; He brings us comfort, rest, strength, encouragement, love, and kindness. In Him, we rejoice, and we trust that He is our wonderful joy!

Daily Joy in my whispers:

Lord,

When we are quick to forget Your promise of joy, we ask that you would remind us of Your faithfulness, and to know that joy will return, Remind us that You see us and consider us and that You understand our limited understanding. Move us to understand deeply that You come to us with Your abiding presence. And in Your presence, may we find joy, linger over Your love, and rest in Your peace. May we rejoice that You are our constant, wonderful joy! With joy, we pray in Jesus' name. Amen.

DAY 9

You have made known to me the path of life; you will fill me with joy in your presence, with eternal pleasures [living with you forevermore] *at your right hand.*

—Psalm 16:11

Rejoice always, pray continually, give thanks in all circumstances; for this is God's will for you in Christ Jesus.

—1 Thessalonians 5:16–18

Fixing our eyes on Jesus the pioneer and perfecter of faith. For the joy set before him he endured the cross, scorning its shame, and sat down at the right hand of the throne of God.

—Hebrews 12:2

DAY 9 – JOY COMES FROM HIS PURPOSE.

Daily Joy in His word: 1 Thessalonians 5:16–18

Daily Joy in my walk:

DAY 9 – JOY COMES FROM HIS PURPOSE.

Daily Joy in my world:

DAY 9 – JOY COMES FROM HIS PURPOSE.

Daily Joy in our worship:

God has equipped us with every spiritual blessing to do the good works that He has prepared for us and to walk the path He has made known to us. Our gaze should not be on tomorrow or the next big thing. Rather, we are to fix our gaze on the path directly before us—where we are, what we have, what we can do for others, and what we can give to the Lord. We can have confidence, knowing that we are on the path of life, our life in Jesus. God has given us clear instructions for a beautiful, joy-filled life.

Some of the markers along our path for a joy-filled life are found earlier in 1 Thessalonians 5. Paul begins by urging us to respect those who work for the Lord (our pastors), to hold them in high regard as they share the gospel with a broad audience, to live in peace with one another, to encourage those who are struggling in their faith and those who are struggling to get out of bed, to encourage those whose faith is small (remember the Lord does not despise small beginnings), to help the weak, and to seek to do good. We are to be encouragers, teachers, "rejoicers," and prayer warriors. Paul encourages each believer to be an "always" person: always rejoicing, always praying, and always filled with thanksgiving (1 Thessalonians 5:16–18). He begins with rejoicing.

Joy takes the burden out of service. So if the path seems steep or hard to climb, if it seems that you cannot take one more step, begin to rejoice. When our path seems hard and heavy, we can rejoice that He takes our burdens and lifts them from our hearts as we pray for blessings, relief, and strength. We come to the Lord with honesty and hope; the Lord meets us there, and we find mercy and grace for our every need. Giving thanks culminates the experiences of daily living. We can give thanks in all things because He is in all things. We find that our joy is in Him, not in the things of life. As each of us becomes an *always* person, our hearts are glad, our words are filled with joy, and our bodies rest secure. As joy fills our hearts, praise flows from our lips. And when praise flows, our problems become small as we fix our eyes on the One who is worthy of all praise and gives life purpose.

Daily Joy in my whispers:

Lord,

May our hearts find the path that leads to You. May our feet be quick to follow where You lead us on the path of life. And when we try to go our own way, would You, with Your grace, gently set us back on the path and fix our eyes on You as we walk and work together for Your glory? And may our hearts be glad and our lips bring praise, for our deep joy is in You, Your presence, and Your purpose. Always with joy, we pray in Jesus' name. Amen.

DAY 10

JOY JOURNAL

Use the space below to record your insights about joy this week:

- What has filled you with joy? This can be a fresh word from your time in God's word, a word from a friend, time with your family, and so on.
- What has stolen your joy? This can be annoyances, arguments, anxiety, or anything that has weighed you down. Once you are aware of these joy stealers, you can fight back with praise, prayer, and people who encourage you.
- Who has received your joy? This is where you get to live out the Joy of the Lord. Who did you encourage, embrace, or encounter that received blessings from you, either in word or action?

Joy fillers:

Joy stealers:

Joy receivers:

JOY COMES IN THE MORNING

Sing the praises of the Lord, *you his faithful people; praise his holy name. For his anger lasts only a moment, but his favor lasts a lifetime; weeping may stay for the night, but rejoicing comes in the morning.*

—Psalm 30:4–5

I love mornings, even Monday mornings. Mornings contain the possibility and promise of a new day. A cup of coffee in the morning is better than espresso at night. Night has passed and morning has come. So often, when I lay my head on my pillow at night, my mind begins to go to work and worry as thoughts of tomorrow's problems, today's sorrows, or yesterday's mistakes creep in. Does this sound familiar? If so, you're not alone. It's hard to navigate these thoughts with a tired heart along with a tired body. In those moments, rest may be illusive, peace may be absent, and joy is nowhere to be found. Tears may flow as thoughts of long-ago flood into that very present moment. The darkness of the night can make us feel as if we are without God, without light. Our prospects seem to grow dim and become more work and more worry. However, the psalmist writes, "*Weeping may stay for the night but rejoicing comes in the morning.*" I love this promise of joy. In the original language, the word *rejoicing* means "shouts of joy, and cries of gladness." Our crying out in sorrow becomes cries of gladness when we find that our joy comes in the new light of morning.

What is in the morning that brings joy? In the morning, we find new mercies and compassion that never fail. In the morning, we find a new perspective. In the morning, we find the Lord awakens us to a new sound. In the morning, we receive new hope, a new word, a new prayer, and new praise. In essence, the Lord invites us to meet Him in the morning. Will you become a morning person with new mercies, a new hope, a new word, and a well-rested perspective waiting for you? This is how joy comes in the morning. With His word open, coffee in hand, joy in our heart, we are ready for the day to begin. Oh, what promise a day can hold when we have joy at the first light of sunrise.

Verses to start your morning.

Lamentations 3:23–24
Psalm 90:14
Psalm 119:147, 175
Isaiah 50:4
Psalm 5:3
Psalm 143:8
Psalm 88:13
1 Chronicles 23:30
Psalm 59:16

WEEK 3

DAY 11

Oh, the joys of those who do not follow the advice of the wicked, or stand around with sinners, or join in with mockers. But they delight in the law of the Lord, meditating on it day and night.

—Psalm 1:1–2 NLT

Let the morning bring me word of your unfailing love, for I have put my trust in you. Show me the way I should go, for to you I entrust my life.

—Psalm 143:8

It gave me great joy when some believers came and testified about your faithfulness to the truth, telling how you continue to walk in it. I have no greater joy than to hear that my children are walking in the truth.

—3 John 1:3–4

DAY 11 – JOY IN WALKING IN THE WORD.

Daily Joy in His word: 3 John 1:4

Daily Joy in my walk:

DAY 11 – JOY IN WALKING IN THE WORD.

Daily Joy in my world:

DAY 11– JOY IN WALKING IN THE WORD.

Daily Joy in our worship:

Third John consists of approximately 200 words. From the very beginning of this letter, we find that John is equally concerned for both the physical and the spiritual health of his friend, Gaius, as well as the church, which he referred to as his children (verse 2). In today's world, the focus on physical and mental health is paramount. While it is important to take care of our physical bodies, developing a healthy lifestyle involves diet, exercise, and strengthening our minds with godly principles. John reminds us that our God is the God of both body and soul. We are to love the Lord with all our heart, mind, soul and strength. John's greatest joy in life was to hear that his spiritual children were consistently living for Jesus, walking in the truth of God's word; he wanted their souls to be healthy and holy. John placed great importance on connecting with God's word, God's people, and God's purpose.

The psalmist writes that our joys are connected to delighting in the law of the Lord. Both authors encourage us to see the deep benefits of walking in the word and meditating day and night on the pages of Scripture. As we continually walk with the Lord, there will be opportunities to learn more and to teach and to share the joy we have in Jesus. We will experience the "soul winners' joy" that comes when those we love come to know Jesus and live daily for Him. Walking in the word is not about head knowledge; it is about heart knowledge. It is about developing a holy lifestyle while learning more of the heart of God, listening to the words from the heart of Jesus, and living a life that reflects a grace-filled heart. What brings joy to the heart of God? To know that His children walk in His word and are soul-healthy. Our joy in Jesus is made only greater when those we love and teach come to know and love the Lord; their joy begins as they take their first steps walking in His word.

Daily Joy in my whispers:

Lord,

May we choose to walk and live in Your word. May our steps be steps of faith and joy, knowing that You guide each step through Your word and by Your Spirit. Would You give us healthy habits of praise and prayer and a desire to study the words of life and the truth of Jesus? May we find joy in bringing others on our walk and connecting those we love to the One we love the most. And may we never grow weary in the walking, for our joy is found there. With joy, we pray in Jesus' name. Amen.

DAY 12

This is the very day of the Lord that brings gladness and joy, filling our heart with glee.

—Psalm 118:24 TPT

Therefore do not worry about tomorrow, for tomorrow will worry about itself. Each day has enough trouble of its own.

—Matthew 6:34

Instead, encourage each other every day, as long as it's called "today," so that none of you become insensitive to God because of sin's deception.

—Hebrews 3:13 CEB

God again set a certain day, calling it "Today." This he did when a long time later he spoke through David, as in the passage already quoted: "Today, if you hear his voice, do not harden your hearts."

—Hebrews 4:7

DAY 12 – JOY IN WALKING IN TODAY.

Daily Joy in His word: Psalm 118:24

Daily Joy in my walk:

DAY 12 – JOY IN WALKING IN TODAY.

Daily Joy in my world:

DAY 12 – JOY IN WALKING IN TODAY.

Daily Joy in our worship:

The psalmist writes that the Lord opened the door and the gates, so he could enter and give thanks because the Lord had heard him. The Lord had become his salvation, and it was marvelous! What a personal testimony to the promises and the provision of God! Although the psalmist is giving a description of entering the temple, we know Jesus is the door to the grace of God—to our salvation. That is indeed marvelous, and we are truly thankful! We know that the Lord has gone behind us and before us giving us freedom from our past and assurance of our future. While we may plan and prepare for the future, we are mindfully present today. We make the most of every opportunity today, not waiting for all things to be perfect. We are to be encouragers today, not when we have more time or energy. We are to share Jesus today, not when we have been trained by our church. We are thankful today, no matter what the circumstance. He has provided today, and He has promised this day for my good and His glory. We focus on today and, in thankfulness and faith, we can face tomorrow when it is called *Today*. We are to be filled with joy today because *"this is the day the Lord has made; let us rejoice and be glad in it"* (Psalm 118:24 ESV).

Daily Joy in my whispers:

Lord,

May we find in today the blessings and the beauty that You place before us. May we see today the truth of Your promises and of Your provision. May we know today that You are with us and be thankful for this day and our daily bread. May we also be assured today that there is mercy enough for today and all our tomorrows. Knowing that the future comes one day at time and that our future is secure, may we find joy Today. With joy, we pray in Jesus' name. Amen.

DAY 13

Light shines [is sown] *on the righteous and joy in the upright in heart.*

—Psalm 97:11

The people walking in darkness have seen a great light; on those living in the land of deep darkness [the shadow of death] *a light has dawned. You have enlarged the nation and increased their joy; they rejoice before you as the people rejoice at the harvest, as warriors* [men] *rejoice when dividing the plunder.*

—Isaiah 9:2–3

When Jesus spoke again to the people, he said, "I am the light of the world. Whoever follows me will never walk in darkness, but will have the light of life."

—John 8:12

DAY 13 – JOY IN WALKING IN THE LIGHT.

Daily Joy in His word: Isaiah 9:2–3

Daily Joy in my walk:

DAY 13 – JOY IN WALKING IN THE LIGHT.

Daily Joy in my world:

DAY 13 – JOY IN WAKING IN THE LIGHT.

Daily Joy in our worship:

Light and darkness. Day and night. Hope and despair. The people that Isaiah wrote about were walking in darkness—walking daily with misery, destruction, sorrow, wickedness, and death. But something changed—a dawning (in the original language, it means to shine, to glitter) of a great light, an illumination so bright and clear that it glittered. How awesome is that? I love glitter! In fact, in my art studio, everyone wants glitter, and I happily oblige. By the end of our time together, glitter is everywhere from the top of the table to the floor; from our hands to our hair, we shine, we glitter. And our joy has increased.

Jesus, the light of the world, has increased our joy so that we celebrate the plenty and bounty of walking in the light. The deepest darkness, death, has been conquered by the life, death, and resurrection of Jesus, the great and true light. He is the difference between joy and sorrow, freedom and slavery, peace and panic, hope and despair, life and death. As we walk in the light, we need to remember that we never walk in darkness. While the darkness may be around us, and we may experience earthly sorrow, He gives us hope and a home. And one day, we will walk into a land of endless day; no night will be there. Until then, know that He holds our hands, keeps us, makes a covenant with us, and is our light (Isaiah 42:6). Just as the glitter spreads all around, so will our joy, even in the dark places, when we walk in the light.

Daily Joy in my whispers:

Lord,

May Your light glitter and shine all around us and
within us. May we remember that Your light brings
joy and that You are the light of life. You have
conquered every dark place and wherever we are,
Your light fills our hearts, our homes, and our hope.
Let our joy illuminate hearts and instill hope in
those who need to step out of the darkness and into
Your glorious light. With joy, we pray in Jesus' name.
Amen.

DAY 14

A person's steps are made secure by the LORD when they delight in his way.

—Psalm 37:23 CEB

In God's kingdom, what we eat and drink is not important. Here is what is important: a right way of life, peace and joy—all from the Holy Spirit.

—Romans 14:17 ERV

But the fruit of the Spirit is love, joy, peace, patience, kindness, goodness, faithfulness, gentleness, and self-control; against such things there is no law.

—Galatians 5:22–23 ESV

Since we live by the Spirit, let us keep in step with the Spirit.

—Galatians 5:25

DAY 14 – JOY IN WALKING IN STEP WITH THE SPIRIT.

Daily Joy in His word: Galatians 5:22–23

Daily Joy in my walk:

DAY 14 – JOY IN WALKING IN STEP WITH THE SPIRIT.

Daily Joy in my world:

DAY 14 – JOY IN WALKING IN STEP WITH THE SPIRIT.

Daily Joy in our worship:

The Spirit of God, the Holy Spirit, has been present all throughout the Bible, in every age, revealing God's truth through His word and through His people. We are first introduced to the Spirit of God as He hovered over the waters of the formless, empty darkness in Genesis 1. God spoke and light came. Throughout the Old Testament, we see the Spirit moving and working through the lives of His chosen leaders including Joseph, Moses, David, and the prophets and through the written words of Scripture. Just as He moved then, He now moves through us, teaching and guiding us. Each day, in every opportunity, and in every circumstance, we have the privilege of walking in step, in rhythm, with the Spirit and seeing His fruit in our lives.

When Paul writes *"against such things there is no law"* (Galatians 5:23), he is encouraging us to put into practice the fruit of the Spirit in our lives without fear of adverse laws and authorities. Nothing can stop the Spirit's planting and reaping except those who refuse to live by the Spirit. We are empowered and gifted by the Holy Spirit. As we cultivate the fruit of His garden, we do not pick just one fruit, we are working daily to have all these on our plate. We serve others with the calm and happy countenance of joy. We care for others with a steadfast kindness; we share the gospel truth as He has been faithful to us. We have a strength that is under control (gentleness) so that when we encounter difficult people or difficult problems, we still point others to His grace. We strive to be self-controlled and disciplined when all else is out of control and beyond our control, knowing that the Lord is not thrown off balance. I am so grateful that this is a continual walk, daily moving a little forward. And if we take a few steps back, He will meet us there and move us forward with mercy and grace, putting life in each step we take.

Daily Joy in my whispers:

Lord,

When Your Spirit moved over the waters, You spoke, and there was light. When You placed Your Spirit in our hearts, guaranteeing what is to come, the light of Jesus filled our hearts. Would You cultivate in us the garden of grace and the fruit of love, joy, peace, patience, kindness, goodness, faithfulness, gentleness, and self-control? And as the fruit of the Spirit grows in our lives, we pray that we become more like Jesus. Give us courage to walk in step with the Spirit, knowing these steps lead to a life of abundant joy. With joy, we pray in Jesus' name. Amen.

DAY 15

JOY JOURNAL

Use the space below to record your insights about joy this week:

- What has filled you with joy? This can be a fresh word from your time in God's word, a word from a friend, time with your family, and so on.
- What has stolen your joy? This can be annoyances, arguments, anxiety, or anything that has weighed you down. Once you are aware of these joy stealers, you can fight back with praise, prayer, and people who encourage you.
- Who has received your joy? This is where you get to live out the Joy of the Lord. Who did you encourage, embrace, or encounter that received blessings from you, either in word or action?

Joy fillers:

Joy stealers:

Joy receivers:

JOY IN OUR WARDROBE

You turned my wailings into dancing; you removed my sackcloth and clothed me with joy, that my heart may sing your praises and not be silent. LORD my God, I will praise you forever.

—Psalm 30:11–12

As I was getting ready one morning for my flight, I checked the weather and learned that Florida would be much warmer than Dallas that day. So, I had a choice in my clothing—either dress for where I was (Dallas) or for where I was going (Florida). So I chose capris, short sleeves, and sandals. I knew that people at the airport might look at me and think, "Doesn't she know it's cold here?" "Poor thing, she must not have the weather app." But I knew where I was going.

Every morning, you and I have a choice of how we approach the day: Will we have the mindset of where we are or where we are going? What will our attire be? Will it be negativity? Fear? A complainer's heart? Disappointment? Selfishness? Or will we choose to be clothed with God's wardrobe of joy, compassion, humility, kindness, gentleness, patience, and praise?

The psalmist tells of the salvation that the Lord brought and how it radically changed his life from mourning to dancing and from sorrow to joy. Sackcloth was the visible representation of the invisible, the internal guilt and shame of being outside God's will combined with the psalmist's godly sorrow and repentance. The word *removed* in this verse means to open wide, to loosen. And the word *clothed* means to belt or to gird up. When we choose God's wardrobe, the heavy weight of sorrow is loosened, and we are girded with the light weight of His joy. What an inexpressible joy we feel when God removes the sackcloth of our lives and clothes us with the garments of praise and salvation! When we are clothed with joy, we not only look good, but we sound good. Our joy is expressed through gladness and praise for His far-reaching love, His forgiveness, and His faithfulness. With His wardrobe, we are equipped with everything we need, no matter the destination.

What's in your closet? I know what's in mine because I know where I am going. There is wonderful joy ahead.

WEEK 4

DAY 16

Yes, my soul finds rest in God; my hope comes from him.

—Psalm 62:5

Be joyful in hope, patient in affliction, faithful in prayer.

—Romans 12:12

May the God of hope fill you with all joy and peace as you trust in him, so that you may overflow with hope by the power of the Holy Spirit.

—Romans 15:13

DAY 16 – JOY BRINGS HOPE.

Daily Joy in His word: Romans 15:13

Daily Joy in my walk:

DAY 16 – JOY BRINGS HOPE.

Daily Joy in my world:

DAY 16 – JOY BRINGS HOPE.

Daily Joy in our worship:

As we trust in Jesus, we are filled with joy and peace, which overflow into hope, and this hope does not disappoint. When joy (calm delight) and peace (quietness, rest, wholeness; at one again with God) are evident in our lives, the power of Holy Spirit is working in us to produce His fruit. The more we believe, the more we put our trust in Jesus, the more we are filled with delight and wholeness; we can rest knowing that we are forgiven and have been saved through His grace.

Our trust in God is not blind allegiance, but blessed assurance. We are filled with Jesus—His love and His words, His life and His light, His heart and His hope. And what is this hope? It is an anchor, an assurance of who God is, what he has done, and where we are going. In the presence of Jesus, peace and joy are found. In His Spirit, hope is found. In Scripture, we read that Jesus is the love and kindness of God, our peace, our righteousness, our joy, and our wisdom. He is our everything. And as we have everything in Him, our joy, peace, and hope spill over into everything we do and everywhere we go!

Daily Joy in my whispers:

Lord,

May hope fill our days as joy and peace fill our hearts. In You, Jesus, we have joy and peace in abundance. May this abundance spill over into everything we do, everyone we meet, and everywhere we go. May this overflowing hope not be stopped by the world's worries or the world's chaos, but may it continue to reach those who need the hope of Heaven, the peace that surpasses understanding, and the strengthening joy found only in You. With joy we pray, in Jesus' name. Amen.

DAY 17

Shout for joy, you heavens; rejoice, you earth; burst into song, you mountains!

For the LORD comforts his people and will have compassion on his afflicted ones.

—Isaiah 49:13

Yet this I call to mind and therefore I have hope: Because of the LORD's great love we are not consumed, for his commissions never fail. They are new every morning; great is your faithfulness. I say to myself, "The LORD is my portion; therefore I will wait in him. The LORD is good to those whose hope is in him, to the one who seeks him; it is good to wait quietly for the salvation of the LORD.

—Lamentations 3:21–25

Though the fig tree does not bud and there are no grapes on the vines, though the olive crop fails, and the fields produce no food, though there are no sheep in the pen and no cattle in the stalls, yet I will rejoice in the LORD, I will be joyful in God my Savior.

—Habakkuk 3:17–19

DAY 17 – JOY BRINGS COMFORT.

Daily Joy in His word: Habakkuk 3:17–19

Daily Joy in my walk:

DAY 17 – JOY BRINGS COMFORT.

Daily Joy in my world:

DAY 17 – JOY BRINGS COMFORT.

Daily Joy in our worship:

In this passage from Habakkuk, we read that there is no hope for provision, no harvest for the planting, no herd in the pasture, and no sheep in the pen. There is no hope for daily food, daily living, or the commanded sacrifices. It seems that the writer has nothing to offer God and nothing to occupy his hands. He seems to only have one obstacle after another in the hard times he is facing. Have you been there? I have. I've had seasons when experiences have turned into hardship, when relationships have turned into loneliness, when plans have turned into problems that seem almost insurmountable. What can we do in hard times? Where do we find comfort? Where is the joy that has been stripped away with all the obstacles?

I am so grateful that Habakkuk didn't stop at verse 17. He didn't leave us with nothing. He gave us the answer to hard times in the next two verses, beginning with a powerful three-letter word, *yet*. When there is no harvest and no hope, we rejoice in the Lord of the harvest, the God of hope. Habakkuk determines that when life is hard and hopeless, he will rejoice in the Lord, regardless of the obstacle; he will be joyful in God, our Savior, knowing that the Lord is sovereign when there is nothing and when there is everything. When our plans fail, the Lord is faithful to His plan. We look to God for His sustaining grace, His strengthening joy, and His saving mercy. He steadies my feet in rugged terrain and in hard times. Like Habakkuk, my attitude in the hard times is one of joy-filled hope. Comfort comes when, with joy, we look to the One who is faithful, to the One who owns the cattle on a thousand hills.

Daily Joy in my whispers:

Lord,

As we experience the hard times and rugged terrain in our lives, would You remind us that You have placed our feet on solid ground and that You are faithful to Your promises? And as Habakkuk, said, *"yet I will rejoice."* For we know that these times are temporary, but Your love is eternal. We know that these times are rocky, but You are the rock on which we stand. We know that You are the God of all comfort and though these times may seem hopeless, help us remember the hope that fills our hearts with comfort and joy. With joy we pray, in Jesus' name. Amen.

DAY 18

The prospect of the righteous is joy by the hopes of the wicked come to nothing.

—Proverbs 10:28 NIV

"Until now, you have not asked for anything in my name. Ask and you will receive, and your joy will be complete."

—John 16:24

DAY 18 - JOY BRINGS CONFIDENCE.

Daily Joy in His word: John 16:24

Daily Joy in my walk:

DAY 18 – JOY BRINGS CONFIDENCE.

Daily Joy in my world:

DAY 18 – JOY BRINGS CONFIDENCE.

Daily Joy in our worship:

Joy is complete in Jesus' name. God's name is I AM; it is inexpressible, unwritten. In the Old Testament, God's name was written as YHWH, but the pronunciation was so sacred that it was not spoken but replaced with Adonai, meaning Lord. In Exodus 3:13–14, Moses asked God, "*What is* [your] *name? Who shall I say sent me.*" Moses needed to know what to say when the Israelites asked who had sent him. Names are important. They contain purpose and power. And in God's loving-kindness, he gave us a personal and powerful name that we can call upon.

In the New Testament, we are told that we can ask anything in the name of Jesus, and what we receive is complete joy. When we speak His name in our prayers—in our painful moments and in our powerless moments—we are claiming His power, His healing, His direction, and His nature. In John 16:24, Jesus gives us the confidence to ask for anything in His name. And when we do, our joy, our cheerfulness will be made full. But what should we ask? Like Job, we may ask the wrong questions or not know what to ask of the Lord. Scripture is full of what we are to seek and pursue. In Matthew 9, Jesus says to ask the Lord of the harvest to send workers. In Matthew 6, we are taught to ask for our daily bread, which is to trust the Lord for provision. We are to ask for forgiveness and the power to forgive, for direction, and for deliverance. We can ask for wisdom, for right motives, and for integrity. We must ask with faith. We ask the Lord to show us the good way and to give us the wisdom to walk in it. We ask for opportunity to share Jesus, and we ask for His strength for each day.

How is our joy made complete? How does this "receiving" joy bring confidence? Our joy is made full by knowing that we have His name attached to all that we ask or imagine, knowing that

He will do so much more with our small requests. Our joy is not so much in what we receive but what we hold onto. We hold onto the hope we have in Him. We hold onto His promises and His peace. We hold onto His love, which dwells in our hearts, and we hold onto His faithfulness that is to all generations. We can be confident in following the Lord and joyful when choosing the way of faithfulness; by doing so, we show others the joy that comes from following Him. Our joy-filled life should be a confident, celebration of Jesus! What are you asking for today?

Daily Joy in my whispers:

Lord,

As we boldly approach Your throne of grace, we ask that You guide our asking. Let our hearts be fully devoted to You so that our desires and requests are faith-filled and faith- forward. May we not long for the "good old days" but seek the good way ahead with confidence, knowing that You have put joy in our horizon. Our future is secure. And when we meet You in prayer, Your presence brings great joy, and we find grace and mercy for all our "asks." With joy, we pray in Jesus' name. Amen.

DAY 19

So celebrate the goodness of God! He shows his kindness to everyone who is his. Go ahead shout [sing] for joy, all you upright ones who want to please him!
                                                        —Psalm 32:11 TPT

But may the righteous be glad and rejoice before God; may they be happy and joyful.

                                                        —Psalm 68:3

DAY 19 – JOY BRINGS CELEBRATION.

Daily Joy in His word: Psalm 32:11

Daily Joy in my walk:

DAY 19 – JOY BRINGS CELEBRATION.

Daily Joy in my world:

DAY 19 – JOY BRINGS CELEBRATION.

Daily Joy in our worship:

Celebrations—big or small . . . the Lord loves them all! Over and over, the writers of God's word invite us to live a life of celebration. However, some people seem to have misplaced their invitation and forgotten to attend. To celebrate, we need a few important details, which are usually included in the invitation: date, time, and place. In Psalm 32:11, we are given the "why" of our celebration, the way to celebrate, and who is celebrating. This is our personal invitation to join all who follow the Lord in celebrating the goodness of God in our daily life. From sunrises to sunsets, from daily conversations to daily commutes, from nightly dinners to morning coffees, we see the goodness of God, and we celebrate. From His forgiveness to His faithfulness, we celebrate. From His generosity to His grace, we celebrate. The way we celebrate has an impact not just on us, but on others as well. Some say that joy is deeper than happiness, that joy isn't seen, and that it is only felt deep within.

In Psalm 68:3, the psalmist says differently. He instructs us to be happy and joyful, to sing and lift God's name in praise, and to rejoice outwardly. We know that what is deep within our hearts will be expressed in our words and in our life. We are to rejoice, sing, shout, and celebrate. We give God the glory when we celebrate all the goodness and kindness He has shown in our lives. And when we live a life of celebration, that points back to Jesus and invites others to celebrate and see that Jesus is our joy. Will you accept the invitation and join me as we sing and shout and praise the Lord?

Daily Joy in my whispers:

Lord,

You have invited us to join in celebration with all those who love You. Thank You for including us in this party of praise. We joyfully accept and will attend this celebration daily. Would You give us eyes to see Your goodness, ears to hear Your goodness through Your word, and hearts that are filled so deeply with Your goodness that our joy-filled celebration flows out into our lives? And would You give us courage to celebrate Your goodness even when there seems to be no good earthly reason to celebrate? May we celebrate You with joyful song, shouts of praise, and even in the whispers of our soul. With joy we pray, in Jesus' name. Amen.

DAY 20

JOY JOURNAL

Use the space below to record your insights about joy this week:

- What has filled you with joy? This can be a fresh word from your time in God's word, a word from a friend, time with your family, and so on.
- What has stolen your joy? This can be annoyances, arguments, anxiety, or anything that has weighed you down. Once you are aware of these joy stealers, you can fight back with praise, prayer, and people who encourage you.
- Who has received your joy? This is where you get to live out the Joy of the Lord. Who did you encourage, embrace, or encounter that received blessings from you, either in word or action?

Joy fillers:

Joy stealers:

Joy receivers:

WEEK 5

DAY 21

An angel of the Lord appeared to them, and the glory of the Lord shone around them, and they were terrified. But the angel said to them, "Do not be afraid. I bring you good news of great joy that will be for all people. Today in the town of David, a Savior has been born to you; He is Christ the Lord."

—Luke 2:9–11 NIV (1983)

After they had heard the king, they went on their way, and the star they had seen when it rose went ahead of them until is stopped over the place where the child was. When they saw the star, they were overjoyed.

—Matthew 2:9–10

Create in me a pure heart, O God, and renew a steadfast spirit within me. Do not cast me from your presence or take your Holy Spirit from me. Restore to me the joy of your salvation and grant me a willing spirit, to sustain me.

—Psalm 51:10–12

DAY 21 – JOY IS FOUND IN GOD'S GOOD NEWS.

Daily Joy in His word: Matthew 2:9–10

Daily Joy in my walk:

DAY 21 – JOY IS FOUND IN GOD'S GOOD NEWS.

Daily Joy in my world:

DAY 21 – JOY IS FOUND IN GOD'S GOOD NEWS.

Daily Joy in our worship:

As I write this day's reflection, it doesn't seem fitting to write about joy and good news. Today marks the one-year anniversary of my daddy going to heaven. This is a day filled with so many emotions and memories, and yet, it is ironically fitting to talk about joy. God's good news of Jesus and the gospel isn't just for the Christmas season; it is for every season, especially seasons of sorrow and loss. He is the reason for joy in all seasons of life. My daddy loved Jesus and now, he is experiencing the fullness of Joy with Him.

The good news of the gospel is the only way to get through the hard places and empty spaces. In Matthew, we read of the joy expressed when the wisemen found Jesus. Joy rested where Jesus lay; the star guided them to the King of kings and Lord of lords. They didn't stop, quit, or doubt in their quest to find the King. And neither should we. Our joy rests in seeking and finding Jesus. Joy is found in the good news of Jesus, the Savior of the world and my Savior from sins and sorrows. There is no better place to find joy. Good news is meant to be shared, expressed, and celebrated.

Our greatest good news is that Jesus, our great joy, has come. Darkness is gone, and light has come. He brings life, light, salvation, and the expectant hope of eternal life. Our love for the good news must be expressed through our joy and obedience. For when we experience the peace He brings, the salvation He offers, the love He gives, and the forgiveness we receive, our response is joy. In Psalm 51, David desires to experience the joy of God's deliverance and a sustaining spirit of obedience. He knows the power of restoration and renewal. We find a "welcome home" in returning to the Lord; we receive a fresh wind and a willing heart. And when Jesus makes His home in our hearts, our hearts are full of joy. Our words and our works are to share His joy with others, to point others to Jesus, and to be joyful (i.e., full of Jesus) in all circumstances.

Daily Joy in my whispers:

Lord,

We need good news, and the world needs good news. And through Your love and grace, we have it. You gave us the gospel, the good news of salvation, the good news of a fresh start, and the good news of hope that resides in our hearts when we give our lives to Jesus. May our joy overflow because of the good news of grace. With joy, we pray in Jesus' name. Amen.

DAY 22

So the church sent them on their way. As they passed through Lebanon and Samaria, they stopped to share with the believers how God was converting many from among the non-Jewish people. Hearing this report brought great joy to all the churches.

—Acts 15:3 TPT

Your love has given me great joy and encouragement, because you, brother have refreshed the hearts of the Lord's people.

—Philemon 1:7

A generous person will prosper; whoever refreshes others will be refreshed.

—Proverbs 11:25

DAY 22 – JOY IS FOUND IN GOD'S PEOPLE.

Daily Joy in His word: Philemon 1:7

Daily Joy in my walk:

DAY 22 – JOY IS FOUND IN GOD'S PEOPLE.

Daily Joy in my world:

DAY 22 – JOY IS FOUND IN GOD'S PEOPLE.

Daily Joy in our worship:

In Acts, we read about lives being changed. In Philemon, we read of lives being refreshed and encouraged. And in both books of the Bible, the response is joy, great joy. The church was growing, and so was their joy. Our love for God's people and our faith in Jesus produce joy and encouragement not just for us but for others as well. We need to be part of sharing Jesus with others and celebrating when they give their hearts and lives to Him. There is always room for one more to know the saving grace that Jesus offers and the joy He brings. I love how Paul expresses the encouragement and joy he received from Philemon whose acts of encouragement had refreshed the hearts of God's people. It is important to see how we can spur one another to love and good works. Like Philemon, we can refresh others. We can speak encouraging and life-giving words to others, refreshing their hearts. And when we do, they are filled with joy, and so are we. Like Paul, we can refresh the refreshers when we express gratitude for their love and encouragement to us. And when we do, they are refreshed and strengthened, and so are we. It's time to serve the refreshments.

Daily Joy in my whispers:

Lord,

We know that we may have spiritually dry times in our lives. Would You bring to us those who refresh and encourage us with the living water through the life-giving message of Jesus? We thank You for the encouragers in our lives—those whose smile can straighten any frown, those who can speak just the right word in a conversation to change the focus, those who bring a warm embrace to the world's cold shoulder. And would You give us the power to be the encourager, the refresher? Help us choose words that lift, bless, and encourage. We love this family of faith, and we thank You for the church. May our joy be found in You and in them. With joy, we pray in Jesus' name. Amen.

DAY 23

For great is the LORD and most worthy of praise; he is to be feared above all gods. For all the gods of the nations are idols, but the LORD made the heavens. Splendor and majesty are before him; strength and joy in his dwelling place.
—1 Chronicles 16:25

For the LORD is good and his love endures forever; his faithfulness continues through all generations.
—Psalm 100:5

But why am I so favored, that the mother of my Lord should come to me? As soon as the sound of your greeting reached my ears, the baby in my womb leaped for joy. Blessed is she who has believed that what the Lord has said to her will be accomplished.
—Luke 1:43–45 NIV 1983

"Then he calls his friends and neighbors together and says 'Rejoice with me; I have found my lost sheep.' I tell you that in the same way there will be more rejoicing in heaven over one sinner who repents than over ninety-nine righteous persons who do not need to repent."
—Luke 15:6–7

DAY 23 – JOY IS FOUND IN GOD'S GOODNESS.

Daily Joy in His word: 1 Chronicles 16:25

Daily Joy in my walk:

DAY 23 – JOY IS FOUND IN GOD'S GOODNESS.

Daily Joy in my world:

DAY 23 – JOY IS FOUND IN GOD'S GOODNESS.

Daily Joy in our worship:

There is joy in seeking God's goodness and in finding Jesus. There is joy over my salvation, and there is joy over others' salvation. There is joy in repenting and in returning. There is joy in the miracles and the message of Jesus. There is joy in God's grace and in His goodness. There is joy in the Lord's dwelling place, His home in our hearts. Where He is, we find abundant strength and joy. When we are His, His strength (to do all that He has called us to) and joy (the calm delight) are found. When we look up to Him, we see beauty and grandeur. Where He leads us, strength and joy are our path. When we stand firm, we are standing on strength and joy. When we think of all the ways the Lord has been good to us, delivered us, rescued us, strengthened us, and blessed us, we are overcome with joy and motivated to celebrate the goodness of God over and over again. And when we share this goodness with others, through conversations and relationships, Heaven celebrates with us again and again. The goodness of God brings joy to our ears, praise to our lips, and hope to our hearts.

Daily Joy in my whispers:

Lord,

You are good, and all Your ways are good. Your goodness reaches to the heavens and down to us. Your goodness is in Your grace and in Your generosity. Your goodness is in the word and in the world. May we see Your goodness every day and in every circumstance. And when we see with our eyes and hear with our ears, may our words tell of Your goodness. With joy, we pray in Jesus' name. Amen.

DAY 24

*Let us come into his presence with **thanksgiving**; let us make a joyful noise to him with songs of praise!*
—Psalm 95:2 ESV, emphasis added

And now brothers, we want you to know about the grace that God has given the Macedonian churches. Out of the most severe trial, their overflowing joy and their extreme poverty well up in rich generosity. For I testify that they gave as much as they were able, and even beyond their ability.
—2 Corinthians 8:1–3 NIV 1983

*Be cheerful with joyous celebration in every season of life. Let your joy overflow! And let gentleness be seen in every relationship, for our Lord is ever near. Don't be pulled in different directions or worried about a thing. Be saturated in prayer throughout each day, offering your faith-filled requests before God with **overflowing gratitude**. Tell him every detail of our life, then God's wonderful peace that transcends human understanding, will guard your heart and mind through Jesus Christ.*
—Philippians 4:4–7 TPT, emphasis added

DAY 24 – JOY IS FOUND IN GOD'S GENEROSITY AND OUR GRATITUDE.

Daily Joy in His word: Psalm 95:2

Daily Joy in my walk:

DAY 24 – JOY IS FOUND IN GOD'S GENEROSITY AND OUR GRATITUDE.

Daily Joy in my world:

DAY 24 – JOY IS FOUND IN GOD'S GENEROSITY AND OUR GRATITUDE.

Daily Joy in our worship:

There is an old hymn that begins with a call, and those who hear it, admit, "We have heard the Macedonian call." Hearing this hymn as a child, I had no idea what the call was, or where or what a Macedonian was. This phrase *the Macedonian call* comes with the connotation of expectation and experience. The Macedonian church's experience of extreme poverty was characterized, not by bitterness or despair but by their overflowing joy to produce rich generosity. How can this be? In 2 Corinthians 8, Paul gives us the answer: an overwhelming grace given by our most generous God. God loves a cheerful giver as He Himself is one. He did not reluctantly or begrudgingly give His one and only Son for us. Out of His glorious riches and deep unfailing love, He gave us Jesus, the gospel, and the grace in which we now stand. And this grace brings overflowing joy, which in turn brings rich generosity. Like the Macedonians, our joy is evidenced by our generosity, and both these traits overflow, even in our extreme trials. Only God can inspire us to give beyond what we are able of our time, our talents, and our resources. Our conviction and our confidence in God will always be shown in rich generosity regardless of our circumstance.

Because of God's grace, gratitude will be a hallmark of our lives. Our daily life will be the altar where we worship Him with gratitude, joy, and praise for who He is and all He has done. In Psalm 95:2, we see that we must also express ourselves with grateful language. If we have a complaining spirit, gratitude is absent. If thankfulness is on our tongue, then our songs of praise will be what others need and want to hear—songs of deliverance, not songs of indifference, songs of gratitude, not songs of discontent, songs of blessings, not songs of bitterness.

In that old hymn, the response to the call was sung back, "Send the Light! Send the Light!" Let us remember that we are the light of the world, and we sing not a broken record, but one that is on repeat.

Daily Joy in my whispers:

Lord,

We come before You with thanksgiving, with joyful noise and songs of praise for who You are and all that You have done. And when we experience extreme lows in our life, would You lift us up and tune our hearts to sing Your praise? For there is always something to be grateful for. With You, there is always overwhelming grace for the moment. Remind us to rejoice over and over again, for You have given us the gift of eternal life, and in our every moment, there is Jesus. With joy, we pray in Jesus' name. Amen.

DAY 25

JOY JOURNAL

Use the space below to record your insights about joy this week:

- What has filled you with joy? This can be a fresh word from your time in God's word, a word from a friend, time with your family, and so on.
- What has stolen your joy? This can be annoyances, arguments, anxiety, or anything that has weighed you down. Once you are aware of these joy stealers, you can fight back with praise, prayer, and people who encourage us.
- Who has received your joy? This is where you get to live out the Joy of the Lord. Who did you encourage, embrace, or encounter that received blessings from you, either in word or action?

Joy fillers:

Joy stealers:

Joy receivers:

WEEK 6

DAY 26

*You have made known to me the path of life; you fill
me with joy in your presence, with eternal pleasures
[living with you forevermore!] at your right hand.*
—Psalm 16:9–11, emphasis added

*A man finds joy in giving an apt reply—and how good
is a timely word.*
—Proverbs 15:23

*Gracious words are a honeycomb, sweet to the soul
and healing to the bones.*
—Proverbs 16:24

*Therefore encourage one another and build each other
up, just as in fact you are doing.*
—1 Thessalonians 5:11

DAY 26 – JOY KNOWS TO SPEAK.

Daily Joy in His word: Proverbs 15:23

Daily Joy in my walk:

DAY 26 – JOY KNOWS TO SPEAK.

Daily Joy in my world:

DAY 26 – JOY KNOWS TO SPEAK.

Daily Joy in our worship:

Our deep joy is in Him, His presence, His path, and His pleasures. To be filled with the Lord's joy is lasting and unending. While the world's fleeting joy is here today and gone tomorrow, He is faithful to fill us with joy today and in all our tomorrows. We can have confidence knowing we are on the path of life with Jesus. And in this confidence, we share with others the abiding joy from the Lord. One way we share this joy is by the words we speak. As Solomon teaches us, timing is everything when we begin to reply in conversations. We want our words to be timely and true, filled with grace and sweet to the soul. How do we find joy in our words? How do we measure just the right amount of gentleness? When do we mix in the hard truths? We turn to the One who is the Word, the perfect Word. Jesus teaches us to be slow to speak (draw in the sand if needed), ask the right questions, and seek God in our reply so that our words will be appropriate, healing, true, and right. We pause and pray before we reply, so our words become God-filled, grace-filled blessings over someone's life. And when we need to deliver hard truths, we seek God's word and remember that He is slow to anger and abounding in love. If we speak with love and truth, grace and gentleness, compassion and mercy just as He has spoken over us, others will hear the joy of the Lord.

Daily Joy in my whispers:

Lord,

Your word is perfect, flawless, and timeless. Would You give us Your words to speak? Would You infuse our conversations with love and truth, grace and gentleness? And when the hard questions of life come, remind us to pause and pray, for we know that the perfect reply—no matter the question—is always Jesus. Help us to find joy in our words so that others will feel the joy that comes from following You. With joy, we pray in Jesus' name. Amen.

DAY 27

I will praise you with the harp for your faithfulness, my God; I will sing praise to you with the lyre, Holy One of Israel. My lips will shout for joy when I sing praise to you—I whom you have delivered.

—Psalm 71:22–23

Deep in my heart I long for your temple, and with all that I am I sing joyful songs to you.

—Psalm 84:2 CEV

I will song of the LORD's great love forever; with my mouth I will make known your faithfulness known through all generations. I will declare that your love stands firm forever, that you have established your faithfulness in heaven itself.

—Psalm 89:1–2

Our mouths were filled with laughter, our tongues with songs of joy. Then it was said among the nations, "The LORD has done great things for them."

—Psalm 126:2

DAY 27 – JOY KNOWS TO SING.

Daily Joy in His word: Psalm 84:2

Daily Joy in my walk:

DAY 27 – JOY KNOWS TO SING.

Daily Joy in my world:

DAY 27 – JOY KNOWS TO SING.

Daily Joy in our worship:

When we sing, we worship. When we sing, we hold back the enemy. When we sing, we bring others into the beautiful presence of God. When we sing, those who don't know God hear His faithful love song. Sometimes, we don't sing. Perhaps someone criticized our singing, or circumstances seem to stifle the song in our heart. Or we might not be sure what to sing about because the harmony of life is out of rhythm and the sound is off-key and the melody is missing.

The psalmists give us the perfect praise, the perfect pitch, and the perfect lyrics to sing with joy. In Psalm 84, the psalmist is not crying out in desperation; he is singing joyfully for the joy of being in the presence of God, in His holy temple. And when he can't be physically present in the temple, he sings to the Lord. Just to be in His presence is worth singing about. To be in His house with all God's people is the psalmist's deep desire. There is joy in the house of the Lord and by our singing, we show those around us how lovely God is, how faithful He is, and how His love endures forever. Our homes and our hearts are to be filled with His love, His grace, and His power. We sing songs of faithfulness, deliverance, and joy. We sing because He lives, loves, and shines through us. Our singing may not be perfect, but whether we sing to our heavenly Father in the shower or on the stage, it is a beautiful, joyful noise.

Daily Joy in my whispers:

Lord,

You sing over us with a song from Your heart. We read in Scripture of songs of deliverance, songs of praise, songs of petition, songs of faithfulness, and songs of Your great love. May we continue to sing these songs to fill our world with Your love and faithfulness. And would You place deep in our hearts the melody of the Messiah who brings joy, peace, and salvation? With joy, we pray in Jesus' name. Amen.

DAY 28

You are blessed when people hate you, when they exclude you, insult you, and slander your name as evil because of the Son of Man. "Rejoice in that day and leap for joy! Take note—your reward is great in heaven, of this is the way their ancestors used to treat the prophets."

—Luke 6:22–23 HCSB

For with shrieks, impure spirits came out of many, and many who were paralyzed or lame were healed. So, there was great joy in that city.

—Acts 8:7–8

DAY 28 – JOY KNOWS TO SHARE.

Daily Joy in His word: Luke 6:22–23

Daily Joy in my walk:

DAY 28 – JOY KNOWS TO SHARE.

Daily Joy in my world:

DAY 28 – JOY KNOWS TO SHARE.

Daily Joy in our worship:

How do we rejoice in persecution? The key to rejoicing in persecution is to remember Jesus' words. In John, Jesus says, *"Just remember, when the unbelieving world hates you, they first hated me"* (John 15:18 TPT). In Luke, Jesus reminds us to not be surprised in times of rejection but to remember that we are blessed. We become more like Jesus when we face rejection, insults, and difficulties. He set the joy of Heaven before Him as He endured the cross. We set the joy of Jesus before us as we endure the critics. We are called to be witnesses to those around us, to not shrink back or sink to their level, and to continue to share Jesus, even in the hard times.

God has equipped us with everything we need to share His gift of grace, Jesus. Each of us is uniquely gifted to share Jesus in different ways—through blessings, comfort, grace, and mercy; through generosity and kindness; through teaching and sharing the truth of His word. We do all this and more, in love even when there are those who reject us, exclude us, and perhaps hate us. Even through persecution, unrest, and difficulties, we are called to bring hope and healing by sharing the gospel, praying in all things, doing good in action and attitude, and speaking blessings and the truth about Jesus to others. There is joy in the hope we have received, and now we are called to share that joyful hope with others. God is working whether in peaceful times or persecution. Let us joyfully continue to work with Him to bring others to Jesus, our peace and joy in all times. May we bless others as we have been blessed by God.

Daily Joy in my whispers:

Lord,

We come to You in the hard and difficult times, knowing that You understand how hurt and persecuted we are even when we have right motives and intentions. We know that You felt this kind of rejection all the way to the cross when those who had seen miracle after miracle and healing upon healing still hurled insults at You. Would You strengthen our hearts and our resolve to share Your life-giving hope, Your deep abiding love, and Your unlimited grace when life gets hard? Would You set before us Your joy, so we may live the abundant life You promised? With joy, we pray in Jesus' name. Amen.

DAY 29

A cheerful [joyful, merry] *heart is good medicine, but a crushed spirit* [broken, sorrow] *dries up the bones.*
—Proverbs 17:22

The jailer brought them into his house and set a meal before them; he was filled with joy [jumping for joy] *because he had come to believe in God—he and his whole household.*
—Acts 16:34

Be enthusiastic to serve the Lord, keeping your passion toward him boiling hot! Radiate with the glow of the Holy Spirit and let him fill you with excitement as you serve him.
—Romans 12:11 TPT

Serve wholeheartedly, as if you were serving to the Lord, not people, because you know that the Lord will reward each one for whatever good they do, whether they are slave or free.
—Ephesians 6:7

DAY 29 – JOY KNOWS TO SERVE.

Daily Joy in His word: Proverbs 17:22

Daily Joy in my walk:

DAY 29 – JOY KNOWS TO SERVE.

Daily Joy in my world:

DAY 29 – JOY KNOWS TO SERVE.

Daily Joy in our worship:

True cheerfulness and happiness come from Jesus. He gives us joy in our salvation, joy in our strength, joy in our song, and joy in our service. The Philippian jailer, having believed in God, was filled with overflowing joy (the original text says, "to jump for joy") as he opened his home and offered his table to serve dinner to Paul and Silas. In fact, he may have been jumping for joy as his whole household, from the least to the greatest, received salvation. At times life may feel like a party, and at other times it may feel like a desert. Solomon gives us the remedy for those dry times, those crushing and broken times. Sadness and sorrow will come, but they can't stay. We are to bring them to Jesus and then rest in His grace. Well-rested and with our hearts centered on Jesus, we dwell where we can find joy through Him.

One of the ways we restore our joy is to serve. When we take our focus off the desert and place it on the Lord, we find that He will bring us to His oasis, His green pastures and still waters. We find that in serving others, we begin to see the bright side of life as we see how others benefit from our willingness to serve. We serve because the light and life of Jesus are the overflowing joy that is extended when we serve the least to the greatest. We become more like Jesus who came not to be served, but to serve and give His life as a ransom for many. Jesus knew that at times, serving would be hard, but He also knew that it would produce joy in our hearts and perhaps a little jumping as well.

Daily Joy in my whispers:

Lord,

Make me a servant; make me like You. When my life seems like a dry, arid land, do what only You can do to bring me to Your oasis—Your green pastures and still waters. Keep my eyes on You and my heart filled with Your joy as I serve those around me. Place the excitement of Your love in the forefront of my life as I wholeheartedly serve You. With joy, I pray in Jesus' name. Amen.

DAY 30

JOY JOURNAL

Use the space below to record your insights about joy this week:

- What has filled you with joy? This can be a fresh word from your time in God's word, a word from a friend, time with your family, and so on.
- What has stolen your joy? This can be annoyances, arguments, anxiety, or anything that has weighed you down. Once you are aware of these joy stealers, you can fight back with praise, prayer, and people who encourage you.
- Who has received your joy? This is where you get to live out the Joy of the Lord. Who did you encourage, embrace, or encounter that received blessings from you, either in word or action?

Joy fillers:

Joy stealers:

Joy receivers:

JOY IN OUR CELEBRATION PSALM 100

Make a joyful noise unto the LORD, all ye lands. Serve the LORD with gladness: Come before his presence with singing. Know ye that the LORD he is God: It is he that hath made us, and not we ourselves; We are his people, and the sheep of his pasture. Enter into his gates with thanksgiving, And into his courts with praise: Be thankful unto him, and bless his name. For the LORD is good; his mercy is everlasting; And his truth endureth to all generations.

—Psalm 100 KJV

When I was in middle school and high school, our church youth group would sing this psalm. It was one of my favorites. The base part would sing a deep "Praise God" after every declaration and then at one part, we would sing, "Glory, Glory, Glory, Hallelujah." It was an upbeat, clap your hands kind of a song. And I believe we were definitely making a joyful noise. The original melody of this psalm is unknown, but the message rings true today. These lyrics have stood the test of time. The psalmist calls us to action and invites us to be active participants in celebrating the Lord. We are to make, serve, come before, know, and belong. He invites us to enter, to be thankful, to be glad, and to bless. And He gives us the reason for the joyful noise in our lives and in our hearts: It is the Lord. He is good, merciful, true, and trustworthy. His truth, not only in His word but also in His only Son, the living Word, will be for all people at all times. When we know the reason for our joy, it will be evident in our celebration, not just on the special days but every day.

We have seen that joy is found in Jesus, in recognizing He is the One who made us and that we belong to Him. We have found joy in His goodness and in His grace:

- We know that joy is audible: We sing, and we shout.
- We know the joy is moveable: We enter in, we come before, we share, and we serve.
- We know that joy is discoverable: We learn more of His love, His peace, and His joy.
- We know that joy is expressible: We thank, we bless, and we speak with joy.

Joy is possible in His presence, in His purpose, in His promises, in His plans, and in His people. We gain joy in our lives when we let Jesus in. We gain joy in our hearts because He dwells there. He showed us that a life lived for others is joy—a little heaven on earth. The psalmists and other biblical writers give us a glimpse of the joy that goes beyond the pages of Scripture to become our songs of praise. When we think of others, look to their interests, give of our time, and even enjoy our work, our walk becomes joyful, and our days are occupied with gladness of heart. We bring joy to God. He delights in us, sings over us, encourages us, and in turn, we bring His joy to others through our words, our worship, and our work. And whether we are in spacious pastures or small places, our reason to celebrate is the same —there is joy in the Lord! With joy, I pray that you will celebrate this indescribable joy every day.

JOY REMINDERS

Below is a list of reminders of various truths about the joy that comes from our relationship with Jesus and our love for the Lord and His word. I encourage you to read this list over and over again, especially when your heart needs a good measure of joy:

- When we are filled with all joy and peace, what overflows in our lives is hope.
- We need godly wisdom to get through the trials. The depth of our faith will either reveal perseverance or develop bitterness and doubt.
- We must have grateful language. If we have a complaining spirit, gratitude is absent. A cheerful heart is good medicine and has a continual celebration (Proverbs 17:22, 15:15).
- Receiving God's peace in Christ Jesus guards my heart in times of difficulty, disorder, and despair.
- Each day in every opportunity and in every circumstance, we get to walk in step with the Spirit and see the fruit (joy, being one) in our lives.

- In our grief, we look to Jesus. In His presence, we find joy. In His Peace, we find courage.
- Our peace is connected to our joy (John 16:33)!
- Be around those who have happy hearts and joyful minds.
- A heavenly joy is not understood by an earthly mind. We think differently now that we are in Christ Jesus.
- Know what is truly important in God's kingdom: a right way of life (through Jesus), peace and joy—all from the Holy Spirit.
- Our outward actions are from an inner attitude.
- We focus on today and in thankfulness and faith, we can face tomorrow when it is called "today."
- We plan and prepare, but we are present today. He provides for my today, promising that He will be in all my tomorrows.
- As joy fills our hearts, praise flows from our lips.
- Get happy here because Heaven is filled with joy.
- Joy is in Heaven. Joy is eternal.
- His words in us bring joy, not judgment.
- God's promise of joy at the end of captivity and peace to lead the way is still a promise we can claim today. When Jesus frees us from guilt and shame, we find forgiveness and joy in salvation. He, our peace, leads the way.
- Our love for one another shows who we are; our laughter and joy show who the Lord is.
- He gives us songs of joy; we must learn the melody and then put them on repeat.
- Be a morning person with new mercies, a new hope, a new word, and a well-rested new perspective. That's where joy is found.
- We have this hope as an anchor, as an answer, as an assurance in Jesus, in His word, in His resurrection: He is preparing a place for me.

- When we wait for the Lord, our attitude is joyful. There is joy in the hope He has promised.
- Praise is *audible* as we sing and shout. Praise is *affirming* who God is and what He is doing, what He will do, and what He has already done. Praise is *adoring* the One we worship.
- There is joy when we read and understand His word. We celebrate with great joy, great food, and great fellowship when we learn from His word.
- Because of this joy, we celebrate with others and are generous with those who need blessings.
- Part of the "joy of the Lord" is knowing the path of life. When Nehemiah read the word of the Lord, the people wept because they had not known God's word and when they heard it, there was celebration. "I once was lost, but now am found."
- Even through sorrow, we have a purpose: We are to plant. When we sow kindness, generosity, hospitality, and Jesus in our times of struggle, the Lord will bring the harvest, and we will see the goodness of the ultimate gardener. He restores, redeems, and returns joy to us.
- If we do not sow in times of sorrow, we will not reap joy.
- Be ready for the restoration! Be expectant singing songs of joy!
- Songs of joy can be praise, worship songs, words of blessings, or words of gratitude.
- Trusting in Jesus brings joy, gladness, and rejoicing.
- Sometimes, trials are in our daily life, and sometimes, they are in our thought-life.
- Satan wants us to ask, "Where are you, God? Why me?" God wants us to answer, " I am not far off. Draw nearer to me. Trust me."

- When the enemy whispers "disappointment," the Lord surrounds us and covers us with His delight. God's word trumps the devil's whispers.
- Where He is, there is strength and joy.
- When we are His, His strength and joy are found.
- When we look to Him, the view is one of beauty and grandeur.
- When we stand firm, we are standing on strength and joy.
- Our joy is protected. Our joy is promised. Our joy is proven and perfect.
- Joy is expressed and is evident in our lives.
- There is joy in salvation, in restoration, and in obedience.
- We find a "welcome home" in returning to the Lord. In obedience, we have a willing heart, and we receive a fresh wind (i.e., new life).
- There is joy in following Jesus. If you do not have joy, then you're following the wrong guy.
- I am clothed by the master dresser—robes of righteousness; garments of salvation and praise; and a wardrobe of compassion, kindness, humility, and gentleness fitted together with love.
- Salvation brings songs of praise. Redemption brings rejoicing.
- When anxious thoughts multiply, we replace them with comfort from His word.
- No one is ever joyful in the dark; light brings joy! Jesus is the light of the world and as followers and friends of Jesus, we, too are the light.
- We look to God for sustenance, for strengthening, and for saving. He steadies my feet, safely and securely, even in rugged terrain.

- He is sovereign over my life whether I have nothing or everything.
- We sing and are steadfast because He is faithful, and His love is far-reaching.
- The weight of sorrow is loosened, and I am girded (i.e., strengthened) with the light weight of His joy.

We find Joy...
- in God's presence
- in the Hope of Heaven
- in the morning
- in His protection
- in faith that my name is written in Heaven
- in trusting Him.

We joyfully give thanks to God, the Father.

God qualifies me. I cannot earn my inheritance. I cannot work my way into the family.

> Joy is audible: We shout, we sing.
> Joy is moveable: We enter; we come before Him.
> Joy is discoverable: We learn more about His love.
> Joy is expressible: We thank; we bless.
> Joy is possible in His presence, in His place, in His purpose, in His promises, in His plans, and in His people.
> Whether in spacious pastures or small places, there is joy in the Lord.

Joy is found in Him and in recognizing that He is the One who made us. We belong to Him and are anchored in His goodness and love, in His presence, in His place, and in the privilege of entering His courts.

ACKNOWLEDGMENTS

To you dear reader: Thank you for trusting me with your time and attention as together, we discovered and received His joy in our every day. I pray that joy has filled your heart as it has mine.

To the wonderful team at Lucid Publishing: They say, "the *third time's a charm*." Thank you for the joy that allows me to share once again from the pages of my notes and take them to the pages we hold in our hand. Together, we spread joy beyond the pages.

To Jennifer and the amazing staff at The Serving Cafe in West Branch, Iowa: I received a warm welcome each morning as I sat by the window, setting up my laptop, spreading my notes and my Bible across the table while you were setting tables for every friend who walked through your door. Although it looked like you were just serving breakfast and pouring coffee, I know you were serving joy and grace that nourished our souls.

To the wonderful women who come ready to celebrate with me the joy found in the Lord and in one another. I am so grateful that the Lord fills our lives with good things. My home and heart are filled with joy, glitter, and grace when y'all walk through my door.

To my family and friends: My heart overflows with joy when I think of all the encouragement, love, and support you have given to me. Thank you for speaking blessings over my life and believing in me.

To my mom: I have known joy all my life as I have watched and learned as you made our home a joy-filled one as you and daddy brought joy into your marriage and as you continue to see the joy in every day. Thank you for this lifelong lesson: The joy in our life is in the Lord.

To Morgan, Savannah, and Presleigh: You are my joy and my delight. My life if fuller and richer because God gave me three beautiful bundles of joy. Being your mom has been one of the greatest joys of my life, and I am so grateful there is no time limit on motherhood. My joy in you will be forever and always.

To my grandchildren: The Lord knew that we would need reminders of the pure joy that comes with discoveries made by little hands and little feet. May your joy be found in the discovery of the Lord and His love for you.

As I write these acknowledgments, I want to leave you with one more joy the Lord gives to you and to me. For all those who are settled in Heaven—for my Daddy and all those who have gone before, I have learned that although we are physically separated, we still can do some things together. We all sing and praise the Lord. We still lean on God's word as it stands in the heavens and is eternal. We receive His far-reaching love that reaches to the heavens and down to us. We are always in the presence of His love. And that fills my heart with joy.

And finally, to the most important person in my life, Jesus, the One who created me, called me and completes me with His joy. I am forever grateful for Your saving grace and strengthening joy that equips me to follow You, for Your far-reaching love that drew me from the deep and placed my feet on Your steady path, for Your abiding presence, and for Your certain promises. My life is filled with joy that can only come from You. I cannot walk this life without you, Jesus; You are my joy. May I celebrate You every day and in every way.

www.ingramcontent.com/pod-product-compliance
Lightning Source LLC
Chambersburg PA
CBHW071950090426
42740CB00011B/1887